Securing the Keys

Lessons on Trusting Your Process
and Pushing Through Towards Purpose

Carleka Spann

www.nuancepublishing.com

Copyright © 2017 by Carleka Spann

All rights reserved. No part of this book may be reproduced in any form or by any electronic or mechanical means, including information storage and retrieval systems, without written permission from the publisher or author, except in the case of a reviewer, who may quote brief passages embodied in critical articles or in a review.

Table of Contents

Preface v

Dedication vii

Chapter One
Getting Out of Reverse 1

Chapter 2
Re-Adjust Your Mirrors 15

Chapter 3
Respect Your Transportation 23

Chapter 4
Securing the Keys 33

Chapter 5
No Car Jacking Allowed 47

Chapter 6
Running on E 53

Chapter 7
Buckle Up and Drive 67

Preface

In life, we all go through some things that seem to be unexplainable, overwhelming or even impossible to deal with and overcome. In those times, it's very satisfying to vent, cry out, or even be angry. Being in a place of confusion would fall under this category also. Unfortunately, many people get stuck in these emotions after dealing with certain disappointments and never move past that "thing", that pain, or that struggle. As a young woman, I fit that description to a "t". As strong as I was, I still found myself stuck. I actually had the nerve to downplay my power and minimize my greatness. All because I was either angry at what someone else did, or wanted to call all the shots, and not allow God to order my steps. Becoming comfortable in a place of "stuck", can be a dangerous thing… and believe it or not; it's a choice.

The many phases and lessons on choosing to win are revealed in each chapter, as well as the results of what happens when obedience becomes a priority in your life. Obedience is so much better than sacrifice. Each chapter offers a new stepping stone on how to get unstuck, how to stand in your own power, and how to win… in any situation.

Over the course of my life, I learned how to "manage" painful issues, and often found myself mismanaging my love for self. I run into so many women (men too, but mostly women), who have become victims of the past and certified "bag ladies". So, I wanted to share more than a glimpse of my story. I wanted to include steps to a way out. I wanted to include what happens when you die to yourself, and release everything that is weighing you down.

This is not a message for the moment, and it's so much more than a boost of encouragement. I give you some powerful tools that will carry you through, for the rest of your life. These keys will enable you to win on every level, if you choose to. It's a little bit about me, and a whole lot of God, that's laced with some life lessons and the power of pressing through. Get ready!

DEDICATION

All things beautiful, that's what she is. We make eye contact and laugh in the most gut busting forms that I've ever experienced. For no reason at all. It's crazy really, because we only see one another a few times a year. Our connection is the realest. A no judgement zone accompanied by perfect peace. She pours her heart and soul into each visit, each conversation. She pours her heart and soul into life and I'm smiling right now just thinking about her. It's been a while, but for her, I can wait. Until then, I'll hold on to every single memory, and relive them again, and again, and again.

And again.

This one is for you, Mia. Keep fighting.

CHAPTER ONE
Getting Out of Reverse

On the brink of the 4th of July, many years ago, I can remember every detail just like it happened yesterday. It was one of the hottest summers of my childhood, and I was at a friend's house having the time of my life. One of my best friends, Isha, invited the whole crew over for a get together at her place. We were all only about thirteen at the time, and the week of the 4th was one of our summer highlights. We needed to shop for outfits to wear to the carnival, talk to our parents about transportation plans, and we also needed to decide who was responsible for bringing a camera... because pictures were a priority for this week. All of my close friends were at Isha's. Her mother had even allowed us to invite our "boyfriends" over to hang out for few hours. Mrs. Garrett, Isha's mother, was one of the coolest mom's I knew. She loved us all like we were her own. We played loud music, dabbled in some make up, (which none of us knew how to appropriately apply), and goofed around for hours. I truly loved my circle of friends. I was never ready to leave when it was time to go. We had a beautiful bond, that I will always treasure.

Everyone was making plans to spend the night at Isha's, but I was not allowed to. My mother was in the hospital at the time. She had recently gave birth to my baby sister, Dae'Sha, a few weeks prior. She then had to be hospitalized for some complications she incurred. With two younger sisters at home, one of which was a newborn, my step-father needed some assistance caring for them. I begged him to let me stay overnight, or even a little while longer, but my plea fell on deaf ears. I was angry, because he was normally so cool about allowing me to stay out a little later than usual. He was always able to talk my mom into letting me stay overnight with friends, because she really didn't like me to stay at other people's homes often. Nevertheless, I just knew I was going to miss out on something major and exciting. I said my goodbye's, while in full "pouting mode", and headed home.

I didn't live far from Isha, and I made this walk a thousand times before. Family members, other friends, and nosey neighbors, laced the pathway from my home to hers, and there was never a stranger in sight. Never. Centralia was the kind of town where everybody knew everybody when I was a child. It seemed as though almost everyone was related as well. I was going to take my time on this walk, because I was still upset about not being allowed to stay overnight with my friends. During the day, you could actually walk about two blocks from Isha's, stand at the corner near a bar called Scotties, and see my home...which was only about five blocks away. Not tonight, however. It was too dark. There were less cars in motion, no one roamed the sidewalks, and I didn't see anyone sitting on their porches. It was a bit unusual.

Before making it to the safety of my own home, I had an encounter with someone. (For the sake of privacy, I will not use his real name and will refer to him as "Kane"). I felt like I was dreaming by the way that I was approached by Kane. I knew him very well. I loved and trusted him. I wasn't exactly sure about what was going on as he approached me. Before I knew it, he was grabbing me by my arms and dragging me. My knees were bent and my body was slouched... like that of a child's who was refusing to leave the candy aisle in a grocery store. Again, I felt as though I was dreaming. It was too late to run. The only thing I could think of, was who in the world would even be able to help me or hear me if I scream. The streets were full of a painful silence.

My body was continuously moving, but not willingly. I remember being asked, "Are you scared?" several times as he pulled on me and tugged at my shorts. I was scared to death, because I didn't understand why this was happening. Physically, I knew I could not overpower him. So, what was I going to do? Those were literally my thoughts. "What in the hell am I going to do?"

Kane had a history with drug addiction at the time. He had been dealing with this addiction for several years, so maybe he was high. Maybe he was coming down off of a high, because he stopped making his aggressive sexual advances all of a sudden. Just like that, he stopped. He certainly didn't stop, because I asked him to. He stopped like he hadn't just drug me nearly fifty feet, as if I was a rag doll or an animal. It had to be God. While I am thankful that I wasn't left with any physical damage, the mental scars took years to heal. What started off as one of the best nights of my life and a night full of fun and innocence, ended up being a nightmare. In the blink of an eye, my life as I knew it was over.

I held on to that night tight, like a clutched fist. It was embedded in my mind for years to come. It eventually started to negatively affect my relationships, my ability to trust, my parenting, and my marriage. I carried that night with me everywhere I went, but to look at me, you would never know. While I wore the pain very well, I had no idea of what to do with it. I had no idea of how to handle those who knew, as well as those I told and didn't do a damn thing about it. What I did know, was that I was not going to allow anyone else who *supposedly* loved me, to hurt "me"… at least not before I could hurt them. Hurting people was not my angle, but I was just not going to allow it to happen to me first. Not again. Never. In my mind, I felt as if someone who is supposed to love and protect me would harm me in such a devastating way, then surely I better watch out for everyone else. The wall was built.

For years, I carried unforgiveness around in my heart. I ended up feeling like the world owed me something…

certain people owed me something… I didn't truly realize that I was allowing that pain, that situation, and unforgiveness, to control me. I mean, I accomplished some pretty amazing things as I grew up and became a young woman. I guess I was what you would call "popular" in high school. I was involved in clubs, sports, and loved being around my friends and associates. I was on the homecoming court in high school, continued to hang out with my friends like a normal teenager would, dated, graduated, and headed off to college. Pageantry was my thing for years. I was crowned Miss Black Southern Illinois, Miss Centroplex Texas, and was even in the preliminary finals for Miss Illinois. So, my point is, while I harbored unforgiveness, I was still able to accomplish much. Something was missing though. There was an emptiness inside of me that I couldn't shake, no matter how much I seemed to accomplish.

It wasn't until I was in my late twenties, that I began to recognize who I truly was. (Not what I could *do*, but who I was as a woman.) And it wasn't until I was in my early thirties, that I truly began to recognize how powerful I was and where my help came from. I turned my pain over to God. I asked Him to remove all the hurt and pain from my past. I had a conversation with the Lord, and told him that I sincerely wanted to forgive Kane for his actions. I wanted to just let it all go, so that I could begin walking in my true calling. You might be asking, "How did you know that you weren't already walking in your calling?" It wasn't that I didn't know. It was that I knew there was something blocking my power. Something that

I allowed to overpower my thoughts, and on occasion, my actions. Any time another person or a situation can control how you feel, how you think, or can change your mood when you are in their presence; there's no way you can be walking in the fullness of God. There is a release that must happen. I was ready for that release. Finally.

Forgiving my abuser, was one of the most rewarding things that I have ever done. (If you don't practice forgiveness, I am sure it might be hard to relate right now.) It was truly a burden lifted from my life. I didn't even realize how easily offended I had become. I had also become very guarded and insecure in some areas. These emotions, had become masked by my outgoing personality. While my personality never changed, my heart and mentality did. I had become a prisoner in my own mind, all because of what someone else did. I was actually punishing myself for no reason. Recognizing my ability to overcome this unfortunate event in my life didn't happen overnight. When I did realize how powerful forgiveness is, I also realized how much wasted time and energy I put forth on something, and someone, so undeserving.

Your story does not have to be my story, in order for you to recognize a release is needed for you to walk in your purpose. Your story might be being adopted, not knowing your biological parents, and hating them for giving you up. Maybe you had a father that was never present, but you watched him raise other children and move on with his life without you. Your story might be a husband or a wife who betrayed you by stepping out of your marriage vows, and left you to start another family. Maybe you dropped out of high school, never completed your GED, and still haven't forgiven yourself. It could be as simple as someone lying on you or stealing from you, and you just refuse to forgive them. I mean, really. Unforgiveness comes in all shapes and sizes. It carries the exact same effect on us all. Stagnation.

As long as you are holding on to the past and refusing to forgive those who have hurt you, you will always remain stagnant in some area of your life. For me, those areas changed from time to time. Initially, I started to back off from church and was extremely doubtful of God. I didn't understand why He would allow something like this to happen to me, if He loved me. I then went running from one broken relationship, to another. All with the hopes of finding true love in someone who I thought would add happiness to my life, (not realizing that I'd never find it until I was happy with myself.) This cycle continued, but when these emotions found their way into my marriage, I knew that I had to do something. My husband had nothing to do with my past hurts, but he was forced to deal with my struggle now, also. While he was very supportive, he didn't always get it or understand why the situation was still so fresh in my mind. For many years, I didn't understand it myself.

Until you release the pain, the grudge, and the past in itself, you will remain blocked in some area of your life. It might not feel like it if you are having success on your job, a house full of beautiful children, a wonderful spouse, lots of money, or all of the material things that your heart desires, but it's true. Many people make the mistake of defining success with money, people, or things. That is very unfortunate. Success is a feeling that should come from within, and it is also directly related to the fruit that we bear. What I am speaking about is purpose. Your purpose in life is so much bigger than you, simply because it's not about you at all. Your purpose has everything to do with serving others in some way. Serving others wholeheartedly, requires your heart to be pure, while holding no judgement or hate towards others. If I sound like I'm coming straight out of the bible right now, it's because I am. The bible clearly states in Matthew 6:14, that you must forgive others in order for the Father to forgive you. I believe this with all my heart and I live by it.

Let's be clear on one thing before moving any further. There will be times that you are faced with hurt and pain that put you in a mental place of unforgiveness. Life throws us curveballs that are difficult to handle and that may initially seem impossible to conquer. So, the message that I am trying to convey, is not that you will never be hurt or feel some sort of resentment towards someone who may have caused you pain. The point is that you cannot set up shop and live there. It's unhealthy, and it will cause you to stunt your own growth. In order to live your best life, you must be willing to release. You must be willing to let your past go, and not harbor ill feelings towards those who have caused you pain, misfortune, or hardship. So, how do you go about doing that?

Step 1
Take your power back!

Make up your mind to no longer be accessible to garbage that weighs you down and puts you in a place of being mentally defeated. Self-love is the best love. Sometimes, you have to remind yourself that God's love for you, and the love you have for yourself, will carry you through uncomfortable places. You must also recognize that forgiveness is for you, not the other person. Forgiveness frees you in the eyes of God. It has nothing to do with giving someone else power. You can only give someone else power over your life when you choose "not" to forgive them, and make holding on to the pain or resentment a lifestyle for yourself. You must love yourself enough to know that sometimes hurt people, hurt people. While what someone may have done to you may have felt personal, it was not personal at all. People hurt others out of places of hurt. Something is not sitting well with the individual who's inflicting the hurt, and because of this, the target could be an innocent bystander. That innocent bystander could be you.

Make it a point to start practicing forgiveness daily. For all things that require forgiveness, forgive! Do it with an open heart and an open mind. Love yourself so much, that you refuse to allow anyone else's behaviors to hold you hostage from living your best life. Post daily affirmations as reminders to yourself about how you can positively deal with people who have hurt you. Keep in mind that you are not required to maintain relationships with those that you forgive. When you forgive someone, you are free to sever ties and are not obligated to maintain a relationship of any kind. This is what some people get confused about. There is no rule that says because you forgive someone, you must be friends or have some type of relationship with this person. The bible does not even teach that. Some people are worthy of being loved from a distance, and this is perfectly fine in the eyes of God. So, forgive and walk away if need be.

It took me a long time to come to grips with the fact that God didn't need my help. For years, I felt as though I was His personal assistant; just lending Him a helping hand with things. I wanted to publicly expose those who I felt needed to be exposed. For years of my life, I did just that. I didn't realize that this way of life would bring more trouble your way than you can handle. Allow God to handle the vengeance you feel is owed to you. In His word, He makes it perfectly clear that He will fight your battles. This didn't register with me until my early thirties. I was running around trying to address each and every situation that I felt needed rectified, while only wreaking havoc on myself. The public humiliation that you have planned for someone else, will be short-lived. His vengeance is always better, and not to mention fool proof.

People who are in the wrong, very rarely see that they are in the wrong, or the damage that they have caused. They never truly factor *you*, your life, or the consequences in with their personal gain. Hurt people are not very logical in thought or actions. Their only thought process is doing whatever it takes to make themselves feel better. You must understand and accept this in all situations. Their actions are not so much about hurting you, as much as they are making themselves feel better. When you accept this, you'll not only feel better, but you'll be at peace, happy and FREE. Release whatever is holding you hostage, and forgive.

Step 2
Stop resurrecting dead things!

Once you have made a commitment to yourself to forgive and let the past go, don't revisit the situation. Remember, it's dead. I don't hang around in graveyards, and I will make a suggestion that you don't either. Allow dead things to stay where they are and let go of the desire to resurrect them. This would be like continuing to pick at a healing wound or pouring salt into an open cut. You will forever experience the pain if you practice these behaviors. There's no need to torment yourself this way.

Remind yourself about how strong you are about the positive things in your life, so that you lose the desire to revisit outdated situations. This might require you to post positive daily affirmations around the house about yourself, and the love you have for yourself. I practice this now in my own home. I'm the queen of sticky notes and use them as reinforcement in my day. I use them at work and at home. I am constantly reminding myself of my goals and my strength. When you are in healing mode, having these constant reminders around is helpful. When you are alone and can still recognize your strength and how powerful you are, this will speak volumes about your growth and how far you've come.

Step 3
You are not your past!

While I have been speaking of what to do when other's hurt you, I am also aware that self-hurt and personal disappointment require the same amount of attention to heal. Your past is exactly that; the past. You no longer live there. So, no matter how many people try to remind you about what you did five, ten, or twenty years ago; that's a personal problem for other individuals. It has nothing to do with you at all (if you have in fact changed). People will continuously go through life judging others, based upon outdated information. We must all accept that. I know it doesn't feel good, but it is a part of life. Your job is to forgive yourself for your past mistakes, ask God for forgiveness, and be free from it.

This also applies to those of you who have hurt people yourselves, need or want to apologize, and ask for forgiveness. Just do it. Don't be prideful. We all have our faults and have made mistakes, so step up to the plate and offer an apology when it is due. In the event that the pain you caused someone else, has put them at a place of distance, and they have no desire to see you or speak with you… give it to God. It's totally out of your control if it's on your heart to make amends with someone, who will not allow you to do so. Whatever you do, don't force it. Offer your sincere apology to Christ and allow Him to handle the rest. (I've been down this road before, and it still offers a true sense of relief and a burden lifted, even though you cannot speak directly with the other person.) If your heart is pure and the reconciliation is sincere, stop beating yourself up. Stop worrying about things that you can no longer control. Let it go so that you can begin walking in your true calling.

Forgiveness lays a solid foundation that will allow you to begin seeing yourself in a different light. It also allows you to see yourself as worthy and powerful in the Lord. Making sure that your heart is right, will allow you to serve others freely and with no expectations of receiving anything in return. Your purpose is all about serving. Therefore, you can't successfully do it with a damaged heart. You can't truly love yourself or others with a heart of unforgiveness, either. So, the release is the first stepping stone. It's the first key to helping you move forward in your purpose. Don't take this lightly. Make up your mind to get everything you can out of life without inflicting self-sabotage. Stop empowering your history. Instead, embrace the possibilities of your destiny. Refuse to take pleasure in being the victim, when it's victory that has your name on it.

CHAPTER 2

Re-Adjust Your Mirrors

If you don't know who you are in Christ, this world is going to identify you as its own.

I spent the majority of my young adult life in broken relationships, and chasing after love. I was looking for happiness in relationships and didn't even realize that's what I was doing. That was my vice, my struggle, my addiction. We all have them. (Vices and weaknesses.) Mine wasn't drugs, alcohol, stealing or gambling. It just happened to be men. I often found myself trying to build relationships with men who truly did not deserve the time of day. I even wasted time with men who I knew were seeing multiple women. Was it out of desperation? Low self-esteem, maybe? No. I purposely chose to behave this way, because I honestly had no real clue of who I was, or my worth for that matter. I also had no desire to be alone.

Even at the cost of being disrespected and settling… I was not going to be alone.

The more I think about it, I have always had a boyfriend since I was in Junior High. If I didn't have a boyfriend, I had a crush on some guy, or a special friend who was a guy, and we spent much time together. So, the truth of the matter is, I didn't really know *how* to be alone. Being in a relationship gave me a sense of security and protection. It also became a way of life for me. I hung around with some very undeserving guys in hopes of my loneliness being fixed. This led to me running from relationship to relationship with no time to heal in between heartaches or break-ups.

By the time I was twenty six, I was a mother of three sons and had been through a divorce. I love my boys wholeheartedly and made sure they were well taken care of. It was not unusual for me to have two jobs to support their needs. However, making poor relationship choices did not allow them to always see the ideal family household. While I am not saying that the men I have children with were bad people, I am saying that I knew they were not marriage material. The chances of us spending the rest of our lives together, were very slim. So, once I made my mind up to end a relationship, it was simply on to the next. My thought process was that I just could not be happy alone. From the outside looking in, I'm certain that it may have appeared to many, that I was carrying myself as a whore. However, sex was never my angle. This could not have been further from the truth. I was simply seeking a sense of happiness and fulfillment in the wrong place(s).

Even as I entered my marriage with my husband now, initially I was still finding my way. I was still learning who Carleka truly was. As outspoken and assertive as I have always been, and still am today, one might find it very hard to believe that I was clueless as to who I was. The bottom line is that I was very much clueless, because I did not recognize *Whose* I was. I didn't recognize who I was designed to be in Christ. As much as I went to church and was involved in the praise dance ministry, I was still settling and ultimately running from the calling that God had on my life. Of course, I didn't think I was running at the time. I would have never admitted to that years ago. I mean, I was just living my life, right? I was just doing what felt good to me at the time. I wanted to be in total control of everything that I did and how I did it.

Did you know that it's possible for you to be strong, but have misguided strength? That was me. Fighting for all of the wrong things. I was good at fighting too, so I did. I fought for the wrong people to stay in my life, just because I could and it was easy. I fought to be in control of things that clearly had no place or purpose in my life, but that's what a controlling spirit will do to you. It will have you stuck in a mess, that you created yourself, and has absolutely nothing to do with God. It will have you turning around asking God to get you out of a mess that you created, only to be freed from it in just enough time to create another one. I continuously fought the voice of God and what He was saying to me. It's funny how I've always been able to hear Him. Even in the middle of my mess, I could hear Him telling me that I was in the wrong place, with the wrong people, or doing something that I had no business doing, and would pay for it royally. I just wasn't ready to listen.

God wants us all to understand that He created us to be exceptional, not ordinary. Every single thing about you is unique and wonderful, because that's exactly how God designed you to be. He created us all in His own image. That's powerful enough alone. It's something that should resonate within you on a daily basis. It should also serve as a constant reminder to you of just how powerful you are… all by yourself. The very moment that you find yourself settling and feeling "less than", is the very moment that you need to do a self-check.

Step 1
Recognizing Whose you are & loving yourself.

You are royalty. Let's just start there. If that caught you off guard, then you still haven't recognized that your Father is King. (He is.)

Royalty runs in your bloodline, so you should act like it. Set the same standards for your life as God would set for you. You must love yourself the way God loves you as well, and not apologize for valuing yourself when it makes others uncomfortable. Loving yourself first, is a pre-requisite for truly being ready to love others and give of yourself whole-heartedly. I've heard the saying, "you can't pour out of an empty cup", so often and these words could not ring truer. If you don't love yourself, it's an open door policy for others to come into your life, and treat you any way that they like. It's also an open gate that will lead to you feeling resentful about giving your love to others, and it not being reciprocated.

Setting standards often requires you to take a step back for a moment. Take a break from social activities and trying to jump into relationships for a while. (& this is not advice to become "anti-social" or "stand-offish".) This will allow you time to do some re-evaluating about what you want out of life and how you want to live your life. A little down time is necessary for that. If you have been neglecting yourself, spending some time alone without a lot of chaos, distractions or requirements from others, can be very helpful. Get in tune with yourself!

Make it a point to have some alone time at the beginning, or the end of each day. It doesn't matter if it's twenty minutes, or an hour. Just make the time. Writing can be a very effective tool when you are regrouping and reconnecting with yourself. Keep a log or journal of what your personal goals are, and how you plan to accomplish them and get there. As you begin to build this list, you might soon find that entertaining certain people or things have been road blocks for you. Writing allows you time to reflect on things that you want to accomplish. It will also serve as a check off list of your growth, and your accomplishments.

Develop a personal relationship with Christ. This is very important as well. You've got to know who He is and just how much He loves you. Use that alone time to include Him as you read your word or just begin to have conversations with Him. (Yes, I have conversations with God all the time.) To be clear, it's not to ask Him for things. I begin and end my day with prayer, and converse with Him throughout the day. It doesn't have to be anything long and drawn out. I just reverence Him, as well as thank Him, for the blessings and favor on my life.

Reading your bible will allow you to see for yourself just how much of a diamond you truly are. There is no particular bible that I would recommend. However, I do like the ones that give you a clear breakdown of what scripture to go to, if you are dealing with certain issues in life. He has the answers to it all. When you're at a loss, and can't seem to figure out how you will make it through, you can find answers in the word.

When you know your worth, there is no one who can enforce a depreciation on you, no matter how hard they try. There will be no one who can tear you down, have you believing that you are not worthy of something, or don't deserve the best out of life. You owe it to yourself to set standards in your life and live by them. Everyone won't agree or like it, and that's ok. This is about you.

Step 2
Don't get caught up on roles.

It's very easy to get caught up in our day to day lives with work, school, being parents, friends, sisters, aunts, brothers, coaches, caretakers, and teachers, just to name a few things. I could go on about the different hats we wear and how easy it is to get busy switching from one hat to another. What many of you fail to realize, is that none of the titles that I mentioned are a complete representation of who you are. Those things I mentioned, amongst a host of others, are roles. In life, we will have many roles that we play as we continue on our journey. Don't make the mistake of allowing a role to define you.

It's not a bad thing to be a proud wife or a proud mother. For example, I know I am. I love my husband and my children dearly, but what if something were to happen to them? God forbid something fatal happen to my children, but if it should; who am I now that I am not a mother? God forbid that something fatal happen to my husband, but if it should; who am I now that I am not a wife? You have to recognize who you truly are in Christ so that you understand you are not "just" a wife, "just" a mother, "just" a teacher, or "just" anything else. Otherwise, you will feel as though you have nothing left or nothing to hang on to if those people leave you.

You are designed to be a conqueror and an overcomer. That's who you are. The book of Revelations clearly states that 'through the Holy Spirit, you have the power to overcome any attack from the enemy.' It also goes on to say that 'overcomers are promised that they will eat from the Tree of Life (2:7), eat from hidden manna and be given a new name (2:17), and have authority over the nations' (2:26). This is God telling you to rise up, royalty! This is Him telling you to recognize who you are and start walking in it. Greater lives within you.

When you understand that your roles in life are not permanent, loved ones will sometimes leave you and positions won't last forever. A better understanding of self will be made clear as well. It doesn't take the pain away, or remove the emotions that you will feel, but it will make it so much easier to handle. Getting clear on who you are is a must, and so is making sure that you don't allow any room for others to define you. The enemy will get very busy when you are at low points in your life. When trials come, the enemy has a way of planting seeds of doubt in your mind about what you can, and cannot do. That is why these steps are so crucial for your understanding.

People have a way of trying to intrude in your life (sometimes casually, sometimes boldly). When things don't look like what "they" have defined as right, they will offer redirection. Some will even have the nerve to say that they are stepping in out of concern or they might even add that "God told me to tell you" line. When you are unclear about who you are, people will always try to tell you who you are. The scary part is, if you don't know, you *might* believe them.

CHAPTER 3
Respect Your Transportation

"Your gifts will make room for you and take you before great men."
Proverbs 18:16

I was blessed to be able to work in the field of social services for over eight years. I have a great passion for advocating for those who can't advocate for themselves. So, this passion has allowed me to work in foster care, classrooms, private advocacy arenas, as well as having the opportunity to work one on one with both children and adults, who have special needs. I enjoyed these positions, because it gave me the opportunity to work directly with people and interact with families one on one. It felt good working for causes that I believed in… not to mention being able to see the fruits of my labor not go in vain.

I can remember working in foster care as a Case Assistant. (It's funny that the position carried that title, because I worked alone with no supervision, but I digress.) My job was to transport children to and from visits with the non-custodial parent, monitor the entire visit and record (or take notes), on what transpired. I also had to share how the visit went in detail. It was necessary for me to appear in court, to speak on how the progress was going with the non-custodial parent. So, overall, I dealt directly with the clients being served. There was no middle man for me. I *was* the middle man when the actual Case Worker, Judge, foster parents, or agency had questions about parent-child interaction.

There was much traveling involved for me. Most of my work was done in the afternoon or the evening hours, because I would have to wait for the children to get out of school before taking them to a visit. I spent countless hours in my vehicle with children or with children and their parents. (Yes, it was often necessary to transport parents who did not have vehicles also.) So, this meant that I not only had to build some sort of rapport with some troubled parents, but I had to build relationships with them. And while I knew that because of the lifestyle some of the parents were living, there was absolutely no way they would regain custody of their child(ren), I never stopped encouraging them. Never once did I speak to them as if they were less than, or like they did not deserve to see their children. My only focus, was to continue planting uplifting words of encouragement in hopes that they would someday want to turn their life around.

There was one visit in particular that stands out with me. I took a brother and a sister to see their mother who was incarcerated, and had been away from them for about two and a half years. The little boy was six, and the little girl was three. So, this meant that the little girl barely even knew her mother, as she was a baby when she was placed in foster care. When I arrived to the prison, the mother of these two children could barely speak, because she was so overjoyed to see these babies. She wept like a baby herself and just held onto them. It was almost as if she thought that if she held them tightly enough, the visit would not have to end. As a mother, my heart went out to her. I could see her pain was sincere and how badly she was hurting. Not to mention, her story was rather unique. She was not a neglectful mother or a drug addict, but some very poor choices landed her in the position that she was in.

I ended up pouring into this young mother for quite some time, as we had been allowed three hours with her on this visit. She picked my brain for resources and possible opportunities that might be available upon her release. So, we planned together. We set goals. I entertained it all, because I believed that she truly wanted to change her life and put some things in place. Things that would eventually allow the judge to see that she was a changed woman. Very few of my visits with parents were this engulfed, but for those that were; I counted it as a blessing to be the person who could assist in bridging the gap on this journey of change.

I loved what I did, and truly appreciated having the opportunity to serve others on this level. I was so passionate about working with the women who showed a true desire to change. And while I had the gift to create and secure open lines of communication, break down barriers, and assist in rebuilding trust between families, this was not my calling. I knew it wasn't my calling, because I had it all under control. Sure, I took some situations home with me at night and cried to my husband about how it weighed on me, but I was not being stretched by any means. I was simply very good at what I did. Very passionate, and very good.

This particular part of my career, along with other roles in social services, was building me for a bigger platform. It was preparing me for more. I knew more was on the way, because I never felt like my cup was being emptied. I never truly needed a "refill" if you will. I could have continued in this role and been comfortable doing so for years. (Outside of salary, that is.) One thing about purpose is that it is designed to stretch you. Your purpose is designed to take you out of your comfort zone. It will challenge you in such a way, that you will consistently feel yourself being molded.

Your purpose also has nothing to do with you. It has everything to do with serving others. So, if what you are doing always leaves you happy, leaves you satisfied, and offers fulfillment to you only; it is not your purpose. Purpose is much bigger than us as individuals, and requires you to walk in selflessness. So, for me, I knew there was more. I was not sure of what the "more" was at the time, but I knew that I was destined to pour into the lives of others, (women), on a much larger scale. My background in social services was preparing me for that. Social services was strategically carving my route.

As my roles began to change in social services, and as I moved from one agency to another, I also began to speak more at business meetings and in the community. Seeds of a transformational speaker, mentorship, coaching, and a purpose strategist were being planted everywhere that I went. It was not intentional. I was just beginning to walk in my calling and my light began to shine in my career(s). I finally got it. There was no denying what I was called to do.

I understood that just because you are gifted at something, doesn't necessarily mean that it's your calling. Your gifts, passions, and career will often provide first class transportation to your destination.

Step 1
Don't confuse gifts, passion, and careers with purpose.

Recognizing the areas that you are gifted or talented in is a beautiful thing. Often times, that's a place where people get stuck. I've heard people say, "I just don't know what I'm good at." Sometimes this is true, but the majority of the time it's not. Most people know if they can sing well, write well, paint well, have the skills of a make-up artist or a carpenter. If not, that's not a bad thing either. Make a list and go over the things that you like and can do well, or have been told that you do well. Make a list of what you find yourself doing often or what you like about your job. Typically, the areas that you excel in are the areas that you are gifted in. It could be something that you have been doing for years or just recently found that you have a talent or knack for. The thing(s) that you excel in is your gift.

Your gifts and talents are also about you. They bring you joy and fulfillment, and you know without a shadow of a doubt that you are good at it. While they might make others happy as well, your gifts are personal talents that you may or may not choose to share with the rest of the world. Your gifts, however, are areas that you are above average in. Your gifts can bring you a nice amount of wealth, because this is your area of expertise. You will find that depending on what it is, people and businesses will want to pay you for the area that you are talented in. There is absolutely nothing wrong with this either. Getting paid to do what you love, instead of getting paid to do what you have to do, is ideal.

Your passion is something that is a favorite pass time, almost like a hobby. It's something that offers you fulfillment, relaxation, enjoyment and happiness. You do not have to be highly skilled at your passion. Your passion is a personal interest that you chose for what could be a number of reasons. Your passion lives within your heart and is normally something that you enjoy whether you get paid or not. It doesn't usually come and go, it lives within you. You can have a passion for singing, but only do it within the privacy of your own home. It may not be something that you would feel comfortable presenting on a public platform, but just something that you enjoy. Your passion also gives you the drive to do a thing. You're always excited to do whatever it is.

Another example of passion would be a man who loves working on vehicles, or project cars. He enjoys spending time working on a car and polishing it up, in hopes that it will run someday. He has no desire to get paid for this, or drive the car right away, but he loves it and spends time doing it often. Others who have a great love for cars might even go to him for advice, ask about certain parts on a vehicle, or what he uses on his car to maintenance it. He might also spend much of his time attending car shows and/or race tracks simply because he's passionate about vehicles. Your passion is often the spring board for your purpose. I'll touch on this a little more in a moment.

Your purpose revolves around service, not you. So, start by asking yourself, "How am I serving others?", and "What do people gain from my acts of service?"

I want to dig a little deeper about careers and service before going further, because it's very easy to get a career in service, confused with purpose. Case and point: A firefighter. We all know that firemen save lives every day, right? Their job is to do whatever they can to save properties, homes, and structures, while also attempting to safely evacuate the people inside. This is such a huge act of service, that I don't think saying they are to be commended would be enough. While this job is much bigger than putting out fires, it is still a career or job. (That I know those men and women do not take lightly.)

A firefighter's purpose however, might be to help people cope with loss, volunteer at a burn unit or trauma center, or even go to schools to promote fire safety. It could even be related to helping others overcome traumatic situations in general, which might not be directly related to fire at all. The point in this example, is for you to see that having a career in service does not substitute for, nor is it always equivalent, to your purpose. I know so many successful people who have found money, but still haven't found purpose. Take the time to figure out what it is and make a decision to walk in it. Once you get out of your own way and make a decision to walk in purpose, that sense of completion will be fulfilled.

Step 2
Identifying your purpose.

No matter who you are, you have a purpose in life and it was specifically designed just for you. Your purpose is the piece of life that goes a little further, is a little bigger, and requires more from you than everything else. It's that thing that stretches you beyond measure. It's a calling that you will only be comfortable answering to, once you recognize that life is not all about you. Your purpose pushes you to serve others, and it challenges you to rise to the call of service itself. Ultimately, it teaches you how to be selfless.

Passion and purpose are interconnected. So, you need passion in order to keep your purpose ignited. Your passion is going to help keep you motivated and encouraged, when things get a little crazy or overwhelming. You see, once you identify with your purpose, it doesn't mean that life will be smooth sailing. As a matter of fact, the challenges will often be escalated due to you being called to do greater things. This is where your passion comes in. Whether you know it or not, passion lives inside of us all. Simply because you don't see it right now or are not being moved to do greater things just yet, does not mean it's not there.

If you're in a place of being stagnant, it's time to step outside of the box, take a look outside of the comfort of the four walls that you have become accustomed to, and explore the world. Explore your entire environment and gain some exposure. Your surroundings will show you that there are more options available to you, other than your 9 to 5. More options than the comfort of your own home, and more options in life period. So, re-igniting your passion will require you to get uncomfortable, and sometimes take a look in unfamiliar territory to see what the world has to offer. You'll find that the list is endless.

Your purpose is your why. It's your ultimate reason for being, living and breathing. Your purpose is so powerful that it should set the tone for your day. It should speak so loudly to you, that you look forward to waking up, and having the chance at making changes in the world. If it's money, people, or things that have a hold on your life, you're cheating yourself out of greatness. Money will come and go, people will disappoint you, leave you and betray you, and all things are perishable. So, at the end of the day, your why is your reason and your reason is your purpose. Get solid on your why and what you are passionate about, and you will have a head on collision with your purpose.

CHAPTER 4

Securing the Keys

Once you have identified your purpose, and have a clear idea about what you were called to do, own it. Start walking in the fullness of this thing.

When I made a decision to get serious about my calling, several people thought I was crazy. I'm sure some still do. I was so radical about my vision and my purpose, that it even had my husband wondering what was going on with me for a while. When you take leaps of faith, (drastic leaps of faith), you can certainly expect people to raise some eyebrows, question you, as well as doubt you. So, get ready. It's on the way.

Almost two years ago, I made a decision to invest in myself. Shortly after, I founded Stir Up Your Gifts. I decided that it was time to stop playing small and just go for it. So, I did. I took the very last of everything that I had in my bank account and registered for Lisa Nichol's 'Speak and Write to Make Millions' event in California.

I purchased a plane ticket and reserved my four night five day hotel stay. This trip cost me about twenty five hundred dollars, which I could have certainly used for the many bills that we had in our household at the time. Now, twenty five hundred dollars might not sound like a lot to you, but for my husband and I, at that time; it was much like twenty five thousand. So, while my husband agreed to support me in this decision to jump, he was very reluctant to do so.

Before I knew it, my plane was taking off, and I was on my way to California by myself. I didn't have a nervous bone in my body, either. I loved flying, loved traveling and meeting people, and was truly looking forward to this event. I had my business cards on deck, took a few t-shirts with me that displayed my brand, and felt like I was truly prepared for all that was in store for me. I didn't truly know what to expect.

The four days that I spent in California, completely changed my life. I met so many men and women, which were already full time entrepreneurs, who shared unbelievable stories of leaps of faith with me. Not only were these individuals amazing people, but eighty percent of them looked just like me. Now, I need to pause here for a moment so that you can truly get a clear understanding of the message that I am trying to convey. For me, as a black woman; It's one thing to know of successful black entrepreneurs, but it's another to be in their presence and actually get to know them. This was a first for me, and a feeling that was somewhat close to what one would call "star-struck" came over me. It was so motivating, simply because this was not an environment that I was used to, and honestly had only dreamt of. Surreal. That's a more appropriate word to describe how I felt.

I was engulfed in a sea of wealth, (financially and mentally). Perfect strangers poured into me in a way that you would expect your mother or best friend to do, not wanting anything in return. I connected with some people who offered a whole new meaning to the word transparency. I sat down at dinner tables, with women who had gone from abusive relationships or poverty to full out millionaires. The funny thing about all of this, is that I did not go looking for the greatness that I came home with. My search was simply to find ideas, and a solid plan on how to grow as a speaker and a writer, but what I brought home was priceless. The greatness was already in me.

I returned home with a new mindset that was bigger than any business will ever be. I returned home with a mindset of "starting where you are." Please understand, that I certainly received my monies worth, but the powerful nuggets that I picked up will last a life time. Sometimes, taking the leap allows you to see things through a new set of lenses and a little more clearly. Trusting your gut, will also allow you to make some beautiful and long lasting connections, with great people that you otherwise would not have.

I hit the ground running when I made it home. I had no time to think about who was going to laugh at my ideas, or who was going to have something sarcastic to say. My mentality would not allow me to entertain any of that. I didn't think twice about the fact that our salaries were barely allowing us to make ends meet. I didn't think twice about my vehicle at the time, which was an SUV, that was slowly starting to fall apart due to being all banged up from the many accidents that one of my son's had in it. Still, I drove it like it was a brand new Range Rover. Living in a high poverty area where every time a gun went off that we could either hear or see, wasn't going to stop me either. These things only instilled a new drive and ambition within me. My calling and my purpose were much bigger than me. So, who was I to make excuses? I got over myself, put my big girl panties on, and just started walking this thing out.

I had no idea who was going to call me and invite me to be a speaker at their event, or for their organization and also pay me… but I began to market myself like I was Oprah. Do you hear me? This thing became so real to me, that I had no worries about who was going to actually show up at one of my workshops. I just planned them, secured the venue, and waited for people to buy tickets. Your purpose requires you to walk in such a high level of faith, that a few people just might begin to question your sanity. That was something that I had to accept, and become comfortable with as well.

What I am sharing has nothing to do with money, by the way. I want to be sure that you don't miss this. It has everything to do with believing in yourself and what you stand for. It has everything to do with believing that if God brought you to it, He will also bring you through it. You must know, that you know that you know, you know. Sound funny? I couldn't be more real with you at this moment. As soon as you allow someone else's thoughts to enter your mind, fear and doubt will set in, so don't. God hasn't given us the spirit of fear, instead He gave us power. (2 Timothy 1:7)

Step 1
Grow where you are planted.

If you are waiting on the right time, the right moment, or the right situation before you start moving in your purpose, you will never fulfill it. When you know, just move. Don't get caught up trying to make sure that everything is perfect or comfortable enough for you. Everything that you need in order to fulfill your purpose lives in you right now, today. At this very moment, you are powerful enough to secure the keys to your purpose. You simply have to be willing to believe in yourself and do the work.

Don't despise your small beginnings. (Zechariah 4:10) Rise up and recognize that your pain will take you to a place of prosperity and purpose if you push through. There's no need to waste time focusing on where you are, because you will lose sight of where you are going. It doesn't matter what your financial situation is, what your past says about you, or who says that it's impossible. You still have a purpose to fulfill and the world is waiting on you to do it. So, each day it's necessary to remind yourself that not only are people watching you, but people are waiting on you. People need you. Yes, you!

Your testimony will change people's lives all over the world. If you allow others to see you triumph over trials, it will not only build you, but it will speak volumes to them as well. Remember, when you're walking in purpose, it's not about you at all. There are some people who need to hear your story. The truth of the matter is, they need to see your story. When others are able to witness you rise above hardship and roadblocks, it will minister to them and cause unimaginable breakthroughs. (They won't always tell you that, but it's not important, because recognition is not your goal.) Fulfilling your destiny by answering your calling is. So, no matter where you are in life, I challenge you to answer your calling and to own it.

It's those broken places that will build you and prepare you to sustain all of the challenges that lie ahead. Everything that you go through in life happens for a reason, but it's definitely not for you to stay stuck. It's for you to persevere and be a witness to others. If you always have it together, never have to struggle, or don't experience any tests; there will be no power in your testimony. It's what you do during the trials and tests that matter most. It's how you handle rejection, having no money, the loss of a loved one, a divorce, or how you handle any low place that will set you apart from everyone else. It will show Christ that you trust Him in all things.

It's very easy to allow your current situation to block the breakthrough that lies ahead, but just because you don't see it, does not mean it isn't on the way. During the times that you are experiencing difficulty, hardship, and are the most vulnerable, is the best time to put exercising your faith in high gear. You must have such a crazy and radical faith in yourself, and in your purpose, that you continuously speak what you seek on a daily basis. You must always speak things as though they were already so. If God has called you to do something, there is nothing or no one that can keep you from it. There will also be no need to concern yourself about how, when, or where. You know, "How will I do this?", and "Where will the money come from?" If God is truly in it, He will supply all of your needs in His own perfect timing. It doesn't mean that it will be easy, but it does mean that God's got your back.

Step 2
Get in position.

This is no time to take a back seat. Once you become certain about your purpose, don't play around with it. Positioning is key. While nothing is guaranteed to happen without error, there is certainly something to be said about planning, and getting into position. You've got to be ready to move when God says move. Preparation is key. So, if the spirit of hesitance and uncertainty has been a roadblock for you in the past, I would offer a suggestion to start praying against it now. Speak clarity over your life and all things that you do. God is not the author of confusion, but of peace. (1 Corinthians 14:33) Get in position and get clear.

I'll start with the mental aspect of getting in position. Mentally, you have to be so clear about your vision, that you are not easily distracted or moved by opinions. Train your thoughts to be exactly like that of Christ. You must be mentally prepared to face lies, betrayal, heartache, and a host of other distractions without giving up. If Jesus had to face it, the chances of these things missing *you,* are very slim. Here's what this boils down to; the enemy only gets busy and starts digging deep when he sees that you are a threat. If the enemy knows your weakness is rumors and whatever the word on the street is, that's exactly where he is going to start. While that was just an example, I'm sure you get my point.

Build yourself up where you are weak, so that you won't be so distracted that it will cause you to have a major setback or worse; give up. You should have a scripture and a plan to resort to for every past hurt or weakness, because that's exactly where the enemy is going to try and attack to get you off course. The enemy knows exactly what will set you off and possibly tempt you. Mentally, you must be ready. Make it a point to stay prayed up. Have a course of action, so that you are never caught off guard.

Step 3
Separate.

This is just a reminder to many of you, but may come as a shock to others. Everybody can't go where you are headed. You read it right, and this is not a misprint. As you elevate it will be necessary for you to separate from some people. This might be relatives, friends, or associates. This process is inevitable. Just because you see the vision and are excited about your purpose, does not mean that everyone else will see it and believe it. However, some will say that they do, but are simply not equipped to handle what comes along with the responsibility that has been reserved specifically for *you*.

Some of you already have a crystal clear idea of who has been, or is actively a road block in your life. I hate to refer to a person as a roadblock, but let's just call them what they are. A distraction might sound better, but it is what it is. There are some people who will simply weigh you down, and get in the way of your growth. Unfortunately, it will usually be someone that you have known for years and are very close to. This will make it a little more difficult to place new boundaries on your relationship with these individuals.

If you have a connection with someone who is always negative, likes to keep drama going or enjoys being in the middle of chaos, continuing to entertain those relationships, will jeopardize the integrity of you walking in your purpose. It will also damage your witness. Not to mention, if you feel depressed, down, burnt out, and overwhelmed each time you finish having a conversation with someone, it's unhealthy. There's no reason to allow other people to contaminate your space in such a way. Cutting people off does not mean that you no longer love them, care about them, or all of a sudden think that you are better than them. It only means that you understand that the calling you have on your life requires more of you, and that you cannot afford to be distracted.

It will not feel good at all when you come to grips with the fact that this person is someone like your mother, your brother, a very close friend or *best friend*. It's so much easier to separate yourself from associates and co-workers, because there is no true loyalty that has ever been vested in relationships such as those. No matter who it is that is causing your growth to be stunted, you will have to start loving them from a distance. You will have to start cutting phone conversations short for some and just not answering calls at all for others. You will also have to start practicing the word 'no', and learn to like it without feeling guilty about it later.

Please understand that this transition will not require you to be nasty, rude, or impersonal. It only requires you to be firm and unwavering about the behaviors that you will no longer allow to overshadow your life, or take up time and space that only causes stress. However, everyone will not see it that way. Some people will take your growth personally and try to place in your mind that you have changed. Well, that's exactly correct. You *have* changed and you *are* different, because you have grown. Anyone who thinks that you should be the same person you were in high school at the age of thirty or forty, is not being realistic. Anyone who thinks that they can continue to be a burden of some kind with no repercussions or no intentions of changing, (eventually), is not being realistic, either. These, however, are not your issues.

Separation to elevation is very real. You will always have to release some things and people, as God takes you higher. You will no longer be able to go everywhere that you used to, hang with everyone that you used to, or behave in the same manner that you did last year, five, ten, or fifteen years ago. When you make up your mind that you want bigger and better results in your life, it will often require you to do some things that you have never done. You will find that surrounding yourself with like-minded people is on the top of that list.

Step 4
Who are you connected to?

Find yourself a mentor, spiritual advisor, or midwife who will push you and help hold you accountable. If you are the smartest person in your circle and everyone is always asking *you* for advice, that's not necessarily a bad thing. It's one way to identify with your strengths. However, in order for you to continuously grow, you need to be connected with some people who are already where you are trying to go. I hope this makes sense to you. You can't possibly know it all, and you should have a desire in your heart to learn from those who can assist in your elevation on your journey.

The best leaders, were great students first. They are forever learning and trying to grow with others, which means that they are not above being students in this thing called life, even when they have mastered their craft and are considered experts. There is always room to grow. So, find yourself someone who can be a sounding board, a prayer warrior, a true teacher, or a coach, as you begin to develop your purpose. Attend seminars, workshops, and most importantly, read. Even if you are not an avid reader, just stay current with what's going on in the world, so that you can be in tune with others and on top of your game.

Your connections will play a huge part in your growth. The people that you spend the most time with, will play a very important role in where you are headed whether you like it or not. So, choose wisely. Your friends, business partners, mentors, coaches, and I can't leave out love interests. The conversations that you are having with these people, are just as important as the conversations you have with yourself. Making wise investments in relationships is no different than making wise investments with your finances. It can be life altering.

Do an inventory from time to time to see how your relationships are serving you. (Don't be confused about this being a check up on what you *can* get out of the relationships, but instead, it's a check up on what you *are* getting.) Are you being consumed by these relationships? Are they helping you or hurting you? How exactly are they serving you and can you visibly see growth? These things matter and only you will be able to determine the true answers. So, again, choose wisely.

CHAPTER 5
No Car Jacking Allowed

Your keys will never start someone else's car. If by chance you get lucky and they do, you will soon find out that you can't handle the responsibility of the destination, because it was never meant for you. So, attempting to steal anyone else's keys will only damage your character, cause you to lose credibility, and put you in the same category as a knock-off. You know… a fake, a fraud, or a look alike. I'll even go as far as to say a "hand me down". This book is about securing *your* keys, remember? God was kind enough to issue us all our very own set. When He thought about me, He didn't forget about you. God loves us all so much, that we all have our very own keys to unlock our God given purpose.

Wouldn't you agree, that it would be very difficult for God to bless who you are pretending to be? I mean, if you need to go back to Chapter two for a quick review of recognizing who you are, please do. I just need you to know that following someone else, because their walk looks glamorous, more entertaining, or easy, is a very dangerous thing to do. God created you exactly the way you are for a reason. He knows that you can change lives being who you are and utilizing your own gifts and talents. Making an attempt to pattern yourself after someone can be a great thing, but making an attempt to *be* someone else will take you out of alignment and out of God's will. There's no way that He can bless you that way. While it may seem to be working out for you initially, the total success of mimicking another individual's purpose will be short lived.

Being inspired and doing exactly what someone else is doing, exactly how they are doing it, are two totally different things. Inspiration is a beautiful thing. There will always be people that I draw inspiration from, that have qualities I want to pattern myself after. I would not be honest if I spoke against gaining inspiration from other speakers and writers. However, you should never desire to change your personality and who you are as an individual.

Yes, it's true. There are thousands of people, doing the exact same thing all over the world right now. However, if they are being true to themselves, it's all being done just a little bit differently, because no two people are exactly the same. Allow your personality to shine through and always be comfortable in your own skin. The moment you stop being true to who you are, is the moment you stop being true to your purpose and your calling. You've got to make a commitment to yourself to show up and own your calling on a daily basis. Embrace your style, your approach, and your look. You were uniquely designed to do what you do, in your own way. God has already set you apart in order for you to stand out. So, don't play yourself or depreciate your value by falling into the role of a carbon copy. If you want to sell out, be sold out for your purpose and what God wants you to do…not what seems to be popular to the masses.

This might sound a little juvenile, but somebody needs to read it in simplified form, so I'm writing it. Everyone is not going to like you. I repeat. Everyone will not like you, nor will everyone approve of what you are doing and support you. So, my prayer is that you have no desire to seek anyone's approval except for the Lords. It's crucial that you take ownership of your calling, so that you are not moved by the opinions of others. That's truly what this chapter is about. (Losing the need to fit in or the need to be accepted mentally.) I don't care how strong willed you are. We all know that it is so much easier to fit in and do what everyone else is doing. No waves are made when you fit in. People are less likely to be upset with you, and for many, you just seem more likeable when you are playing it safe and living your life "inside the box."

As soon as you decide to own your calling, one of the first things people will want to know is, "Who do you think you are?" While it's really not funny, I have to laugh at this. Because my thought is "Who are *you* to question what I am doing?" People who don't like change, or have their own ideas of what your purpose or blessings are, especially what they should look like, won't always receive you well or wish you well. This is all ok. Just be prepared for the reactions of those who have an issue with you not fitting into the cookie cutter mold, that they feel you should.

The attacks on your life will begin to multiply when the enemy sees that you are the real deal, and that you did not come to play. Your tests will increase along with your faith being challenged, because the enemy wants you to doubt who you are and what you are called to do. The enemy wants to plant seeds of insecurity in your mind, to make you feel unworthy and unsure. This is right about the time that it might be a bit enticing to take the easy way out, by adopting what you see someone else doing that looks a little bit easier, and doesn't require as much strength or will power.

Let's be clear on something, you have no clue of what has happened behind the scenes in someone else's life. You have no idea of the cost of someone else's praise or public outcome. Some people have struggled for years to get to where they are. All you see is the finished product or their highlight reel. So, embrace the individuality of others, instead of trying to adopt it. Your true area of expertise when walking in your purpose, will be what you have experienced and how it has developed you. No matter what anyone tells you, you are fully equipped for this journey. Everything that you need, already lives in you.

Step 1
(There's only one step, so pay close attention.)
Rise up royalty.

When you are doing what God has called you to do, it might not be popular. It might not be what's trending or what is attractive to the masses. Chances are, that when you begin to walk boldly in your purpose, it might initially feel as though you just don't fit in, because you look different and present yourself to the world differently than everyone else. Let this be a sign not only of your leadership, but also of your royalty. Royalty needs no validation, nor does royalty need an applause to feel worthy of simply being. It's time to rise up and lose the spirit of wanting to follow and fit in. Now is the time for you to take your rightful place in the world as a leader of your own unique ministry. It was never Gods plan to have us walking around looking and acting alike. It is true that we were all created equal, but most definitely not alike.

Prepare for others to mock you and challenge your uniqueness. It simply comes with the territory. Prepare to stand alone often, as people fear change and differences. Continue to stand in your power and know that if God led you to it, He will certainly carry you through it.

Understand that you are enough. Yes, you. You are powerful enough, strong enough, courageous enough, bold enough, smart enough, pretty enough or handsome enough, to do exceedingly wonderful things through

Christ. There's no reason for you to look any further than yourself, in order to stand firmly in your calling. There's also no reason to search for a substitute, replacement, or what you might feel is a better version of what you have to offer the world. You are fully equipped to serve a greater purpose in life, if you choose to answer God's call.

It's necessary for you to get comfortable with embracing everything about yourself, flaws and all, and understand that what God has for you, is for you. You won't have to steal, beg, borrow, and certainly not pretend, to be someone else in order for Him to bless you. Purpose isn't tied to any of those things. The way that you look, the way that you walk, talk and act, are all unique, because no one else was created like you. Even identical twins have something unique about them, in order to set them apart from one another. Your uniqueness should be embraced, simply because you were designed by God.

Often times, it's necessary to just be still and know. (Psalms 46:10) Know that God is all powerful and the King of King's, and that He will supply all of your needs. There is no need to go searching for what someone else has, because you feel as though what God has given you is not enough. God's not in the business of short changing His children, and He is definitely not fond of the spirit of jealousy. Give God the opportunity to handle your concerns, by casting your cares unto Him. He won't leave you hanging.

CHAPTER 6

Running on E

I often have to remind myself, of how important it is to stay in the will of God. Every day that you go without including Him in your life and begin operating your own power alone, you're taking a risk and operating in a danger zone.

Have you ever had someone "come for you"? You know what I mean… come for you in such a disrespectful way, that you had to question whether or not they were actually directing their conversation at you. It can be very challenging to have someone test your professionalism or character. Especially when you are already out of Gods will, and have been calling all the shots in your life, with no reservation as to what the consequences of your reckless behavior might be.

Several years ago, I was working for a private agency as an advocate for special needs individuals. I absolutely loved my job, and those I worked with as well. That's usually a very hard combination to come by, so I considered myself to be pretty blessed. I wasn't sure that I would be there for a substantial amount of time, but I certainly saw myself there for a few years. It was a small, quiet office, and I enjoyed that. I liked my private office, and the fact that my co-workers and I got along. This job required me to travel in order to fulfill meeting client visits, but that was not an issue for me either.

One afternoon, after returning from lunch, I settled back into my office as I normally would. I logged into my computer, and was caught off guard by a very surprising email. This was the kind of email that makes you get up, close your office door, lock it, and read it over several times very carefully. I could not believe my eyes. Surely, there had been some kind of mistake or something. Because the boss I knew would not be addressing me in this manner. It took all I had to hold the tears back, as I continued to read this nonsense. My boss had already left the office, so I could not address this issue with him right away.

My entire face got hot as I read the attacks on my work ethic and character. In short, the email basically said that I was not doing anything right on my job. At all. It also included cancellations of a few business trips, which were coming up for me that I was looking forward to. I sat in disbelief, as I read the demeaning words that carried a nasty tone throughout. I didn't understand how someone who never spoke a negative word to me in two years, could rip me to shreds in the blink of an eye. Not to mention doing it in an email. I had never been in any kind of trouble on my job, and had been employed there for over two years at that point. I never had one write up, no warnings, and my evaluations were commendable. I had no clue of what this was all about, but before I could finish the day, I left in a rage, (but not before making several copies of that email).

Before I could even get in my car good, I was on the phone texting my girlfriends about where we were going to meet. This was a justifiable cause for an emergency meeting of course. (Mind you, I thought about them, before I thought about my husband.) Now, I don't know what kind of friends you have, but the girls I roll with do not play around about our friendship. All they needed to see, was that I was having an emergency and what time we were going to meet. They didn't ask questions about what was going on, why I needed them, or offer me reasons about why they could not make it. They all replied, "I will be there." Please believe they showed up at our normal meeting spot and were anxiously awaiting my arrival.

I sat down at the table, and said nothing. I pulled the copies of the emails out of my bag, placed them on the table for their review, and just sat back. Their eyes got big, and rolled. They sighed and offered body language that words can't quite describe. They were sucking their teeth and seething more than I think I did, when I read it for the first time. They simply asked, "What do you want us to do?" They meant that, too. That "what" meant they were down for whatever. Luckily, for my previous boss, I was not angry enough to make any special demands of slashing tires or busting windows, because I am sure it would have gone down that day. I was hurting, and because my friends love me like they do, it hurt them to see me in the pain I was in.

After making it home to share this news with my husband, he handled the situation the exact opposite of my girlfriends. He is such a low key, reserved type of guy. He didn't get angry, or raise his voice after reading the email that I shared. He calmly shared that he knew how I must feel, and that he was sorry I had to deal with this. He also suggested that when I make it to the office the following day, (which was when I was supposed to meet with my boss), that I just remain calm, and listen to what he had to say. In my mind, I wondered if my husband read the same email that I did. His words went in one ear and right out the other.

The next day, before it was time for my boss and I to meet, I made a decision to quit. That's right. I had no desire to even hear what he could possibly have to say to me. I was done. Without another job to go to, I was done. Without consulting with my husband, I was done. I emailed my boss my letter of resignation, and in the blink of an eye, it was over. In my mind, I didn't need that job, they needed *me*. I felt so hurt and betrayed, that I could not even think clearly at the time. While I had every reason to feel the way that I felt, my emotions got the best of me.

My husband advised me to go back to the office and speak with my boss, but I refused. He later asked me to call my boss on the phone, but I refused that request as well. (I hope you all are following me, because it gets deeper. Much deeper.) My husband was angry and I was hurt. It was a horrible combination and the icing on the cake, (if you want to call it icing), is that I was pregnant. I was four months pregnant at the time, and had just made a decision to walk away from a job. Let that sink in for a moment.

Two weeks hadn't passed before I started to have a few complications with my pregnancy, and was being rushed to a hospital in St. Louis. Our baby boy was fighting for his life, and the doctors were doing everything they could to save him. I went through a host of procedures, tests, and felt more needles than I care to remember. After three days of procedures and creative ideas to make this pregnancy last, our son went on to heaven. I delivered Christoff, and we said our goodbyes all in a matter of moments. Our precious baby boy would not be leaving with us. There would be no blue balloons or car seats. Just us… taking that long ride home in tears and silence.

So, there we were. An entire salary shorter, still grieving the passing of our son, and not speaking to one another. That's another book in itself, but we were in a place of complete disarray.

A couple months later, I was offered an opportunity to work in the classroom at Mt. Vernon Township High School as a Paraprofessional. That's a fancy name for a teacher's aide, for those who might not know. I had built a great rapport with the Director of Special Education.

She was excited to have me as a part of her team. Initially, after sharing the opportunity with my husband, I was a bit reluctant to jump at the positon. I knew that teacher's aides were paid very little. I mean, *very* little, but I accepted.

The year I spent as a Paraprofessional ended up being one of the most challenging, yet rewarding years of my life. God broke me down piece by piece during this school year, and He made sure that He had my undivided attention. How would my family and I make it on my husband's salary alone? (My check barely covered gas for my truck now.) How would my husband and I pull through being in such a broken place in our marriage? (Divorce was a very hot topic at the time.) I had no other choice, but to turn it all over to God. I was out of great ideas, and I was all out of plans. God was my last and final option. While truly, He should have been the first.

All this time I was running on empty. I was continuously filling my tank up with self and selfishness, that was taking me nowhere, fast. I had no true idea of what it really meant to serve, until all of this happened. I have always helped people, loved working with others, and volunteered my time, but truly serving my family and serving Christ had not honestly been a constant priority for me. It was in this season of my life that my prayer life was strengthened, my marriage began to flourish, and a true revelation about purpose was felt. I no longer had a dime in the four hundred dollar Michael Kors bag that I carried. I was surrounded by students whose fast food checks were much larger than mine, and I *had* to smile and cheer when they brought them to my desk for me to see how much they made.

If I had not been able to identify with what it meant to be humbled before, there was no way around it this time. I felt every inch of my person being molded and being groomed, for a purpose much larger than myself. I felt God pulling, pushing, and simply desiring more from me. I began to yield to Him and just offered myself to Him, completely.

It's so very easy to get in your own way, because you *feel* a certain way at the time. I just want to encourage you to stay out of your feelings, and allow God to order your steps. Allow God to take care of your concerns. When you don't allow God to lead, you end up running on fumes which will only carry you so far. Take heed to God's warning signs as well, because if He has to actually reach out and grab your attention after multiple attempts, well… you will wish your feelings would have had a seat.

The Assignment

As a paraprofessional at the high school, there were two certified teachers that I would be working directly under. One, coincidentally was the same age as myself. The other, much older and the least likely for me to make a connection with. (Oh, but God does work in mysterious ways.)

Ms. Jones was a very quiet lady. She stood about four feet three inches tall, if that. She wore a very basic, masculine buzz cut like that of a military soldier, no make-up, and had very smooth pale skin. Ms. Jones was extremely overweight for her height, and had tremendous health conditions, (which I knew nothing about upon our introduction). When I say we both had a similar reaction when we found out that we'd be in the same classroom together, I mean it was absolutely uncanny. We played very nice by introducing ourselves, making small talk, and getting a feel for each other. However, both of our eyes were saying, "Uh oh, how in the world is this going to play out?"

She was quiet, and I was outgoing and assertive. She didn't seem to have anything interesting to talk about, and I had a host of interesting life lessons to share. She was different in that she hadn't really seen much of the world outside of her small hometown and the classroom. We were simply opposites and I had a feeling that this was going to be a little difficult.

Believe it or not, Ms. Jones and I hit it off in less than two weeks. Who knew that the most unlikely pair of individuals, would end up becoming friends. This would strongly support the fact that you should never judge a book by its cover. You could end up missing out on a world of greatness. Ms. Jones and I had what I would say was one of the best friendships that anyone could ask for. I learned so much about her in a short amount of time, because we ended up spending the majority of our lunch hours together. Because of her health condition, she walked very slowly and very rarely left the classroom for any reason. She began to open up to me about her work and family life, along with her illnesses. She was being faced with so much, that my heart went out to her. Not for reasons of sympathy, but because as I got to know her, I quickly learned that she was one of the most kind people around who certainly did not deserve to be treated the way that she was.

It didn't take long for me to find out that she was not very close to any of the teachers at the high school, outside of about two people, maybe three. Her rapport with others was good, but she had no genuine connection with the teachers that she worked closely with, (not while I was there anyway). This bothered her a great deal, and she shared much about how it made her feel. She trusted me with so much, but her sharing this information with me was just the beginning of us becoming close.

I began to pray with her and for her. She didn't seem to have a close relationship with Christ, but was glad to know that I was willing to pray for her. She was open to all that I shared. I also began to encourage her, and talk with her about having faith and believing in the power to overcome certain situations. We laughed and cried together for months, but this relationship came to an unfortunate halt. Ms. Jones passed away in the winter of the first semester of that school year.

I stayed on the phone with her as much as I could, when she was able to talk during her hospital stay. I kept in touch with her husband and went to pray with her a few times. In a matter of days, she was gone. Just like that, her illness along with developing pneumonia took her life.

The joy in this situation, is that I know exactly where

Ms. Jones is resting. In our short time together, it was made very clear that she knows Jesus as her Lord and Savior and believes that He died for our sins. Ms. Jones was such a beautiful person, and had I ignored my assignment and made a stink out of the connection that God strategically set up, I would have missed a beautiful blessing. The joy in ministering to Ms. Jones, encouraging her, and building a relationship that would add so much to both my life and hers, was simply priceless.

Just to think, all of this came out of places of brokenness. I was broken and so was Ms. Jones. Our paths crossed for a reason that was much bigger than she and I. I was in a place of financial strain, suffering a loss, and on the verge of a divorce. She was in a place of loneliness, dealing with past struggles, and trying to manage some overwhelming health conditions. It was at this very moment that God told me to rise up, get over myself, and start proclaiming the life that I wanted to begin living. He reminded me that I belonged to Him and needed to start acting like it. He reminded me that I was not my situation, nor was I my geographical location, and that through Him, I had the power to change it all. I started with Ms. Jones, and that quickly led to me pouring my heart and soul into my students. (Her students became my students after she passed away, and I was allowed to lead her classroom.)

This was the year of building wealth from the inside out. This was my first season of "the press". I call it that, because I felt every inch of growth that year. It was me and God. I had no other secret weapons in this season.

I had no one to call to get me out of this jam and save the day. I'm sure no one would have been successful with the rescue, even if I did. God had another plan for me. I literally pressed my way through, by helping someone else. I pressed my way through, by being willing to accept my assignment. I stopped trying to fix everything on my own, call all the shots, and allowed God to have His way, (without a fight), for the first time in my life.

In life, you will have many assignments. In order to recognize them when they show up, you must be willing to get out of your own way, and trust God to order your steps. He will create an assignment for you as soon as you get comfortable, feel like it's time to take a break, or of course, are in a place of disobedience. Much like your purpose, your assignments will stretch you. They are not designed to feel good or glorify you. It's all about Him.

Step 1
Use your gas cards.

It's mandatory that you stay prayed up, and do your best to walk and live in God's will. As soon as you stray from either, you'll find your tank much closer to E and possibly more difficult to fill. While God has been kind enough to issue you the keys, it's your responsibility to keep your tank full. The only way to do this, is to die to yourself, and walk away from any selfish ways. What good will having the keys do if you're attempting to drive on fumes?

Stay in His word, so that you are always prepared for anything that life throws your way. Staying in His word and will do not offer you a guarantee of not facing trials, but it does guarantee that you will be covered and remain a conqueror in all things. When you are out of the will of the Lord, you forfeit your right to call Him your protector. Luke 9:23

I know that it can be hard to walk away from your own ideas and plans at times. Especially if you feel as though God has forgotten you, or if things aren't happening as fast as you would like for them to. Just keep in mind that God is not a "right now" God, He's an on time God and He will never fail you. He is always setting you up for victory. You have to trust and believe that at all times. The set up can be a beautiful thing, if you are willing to endure the trials for a season.

Step 2
Accept the assignment.

God wants to give you beauty for ashes. He wants to mend those broken places and rebuild them. Even when you can't see the glory in a situation, God does.

Just like you should not despise your small beginnings, you should not frown upon an assignment, just because it doesn't appear glamorous or doesn't look enjoyable. I learned about the beauty of dark places the hard way. I am sharing this, so that hopefully you can get it, without having to go through as many rough patches as I did. Your obedience to answering God's call, is going to play a major part in the outcome of your story. Understand that there are no short cuts and no passes on yielding to an assignment. The lesson is always in following through.

There is so much power and potential that can be unlocked, by accepting your assignment. All you have to do, is say yes. You don't need any extra assistance or specialized training, no degrees or long list of accolades to fulfill the assignments that God places before you. He has given you everything you need in order to fulfill your assignment. And while you are the one fulfilling the assignment, there is a one hundred percent chance that the lives of others will be changed, become richer, and be blessed because of your willingness to complete it. See how this is connected to purpose? It's all very closely intertwined. Live a more abundant life, by following through with the assignment.

CHAPTER 7

Buckle Up and Drive

When you know where you're headed and allow God to lead the way, there won't be any person or situation that can stand in your way and cause hesitation. Worry, nor doubt, will even be able to set in on your journey.

I can remember very clearly, the day that a gentleman came into the office that I currently work in. He thought it was necessary to question my location in the office. He was a very nice man that does business with the high school, and his approach was not rude or disrespectful in any way. He did, however, find it very strange that it was not me, (the Executive Assistant), that he saw in the front window, seated at the front desk greeting him when he arrived. As he was led back to my office space, I am sure he had only one question on his mind, because it was the first thing that popped out of his mouth, when he reached me. He said, "Why are you all the way in the back? Shouldn't you be at the front desk? Why aren't you in the front where everyone can see you?" I just smiled and offered him a very clear, yet professional response.

I shared with him that there was a receptionist desk in the front for a reason. The front of the office sits at the entrance of the building, which at times is highly trafficked. That leaves room for the possibility of many distractions, as well as a disconnection with the Superintendent, who is my boss. I shared with him that the Superintendent's office is in the back also, not just mine. In order for our working relationship to be as seamless as it is, it works best if we are physically located in the same place.

I don't need to be seen in order to do what I do, and I never thought twice about my location prior to this particular man coming in and questioning it. What's funny is that many staff members began to question it soon after as well. My location has everything to do with me being on my "A game", at all times. I am in a low traffic area, with minimal noise, and no distractions outside of the phone. Our office is also set up to where someone else is in a position to run interference with the public and visitors *before* they even reach us.

This set up reminds me so much of how God loves and cares for us. He has a way of placing a hedge of protection around us, in order to make sure that we are not thrown off course. You see, being in the front is sometimes the worst place to be depending on the situation. If that's where I was *supposed* to be, that's where I would be. Don't allow anyone to come in and challenge your position on your journey, simply because it does not add up to them.

The point here, is that people will always have an opinion about where you should be in life, based upon their own personal thoughts. They will also have this ridiculous idea that it is necessary for you to be seen in order to accomplish things or achieve your goals. When the man began to speak about where I was positioned, I just thought about how I was currently accomplishing more work behind the scenes, than I probably have before in my life. Being front and center or being first carry no weight on the fulfillment of your purpose. Making it a point to stay focused and staying the course is what matters. This is not a race or a competition.

There is no need to be in a hurry, or become upset about where you might currently be. Trusting your own process is what will carry you through. There is no way that you should compare where you are on your journey with where someone else may be. Just drive. There is a reason that the navigation of your process is set up the way that it is, also. It's about making sure that you get there. It's not about how fast you're going or who can see you along the way. Someone being blessed or encouraged by being able to witness what happens on your journey is one thing, but the plan is certainly not to entertain or receive validation from anyone.

It's so important that you get into a mindset of believing in yourself, especially on your worst days. You know, those days when the enemy decides to rear his ugly head and spew out lies about how you will never make it or how it's impossible. Well, let me let you in on a little secret. If you give up, the enemy will be absolutely correct and you might as well throw your keys away. Don't ever allow anyone else to tell you what you can't do. This world is full of dream killers who try to do everything in their power to discourage and tear down the plans that others have. However, just because they are talking does not mean that you are obligated to listen.

When you are faced with the questions and challenges about why you are where you are on your journey, you just keep driving. An explanation is never necessary unless you choose for it to be. You always have choices. You can choose to entertain doubt, fear, and the inquisitive minds of people all day long, and it won't get you anywhere, but stuck. You can never truly walk in your purpose, if you're trying to bring anything along that God did not authorize to come with you. Doubt, fear, and opinions, are on the top of that list.

Step 1
Pack light.

Clear your mind of any negative thoughts that might stand in the way of you fulfilling your calling and your purpose. It's true, that your thoughts become words and your words become actions. If you're not careful about who you're listening to, you might soon start to believe doubtful words. Before you know it, those negative seeds have begun to grow within you. Stand firm on where you're headed, and confident about the transportation in which God has given you to arrive.

Someone is always going to have something to say about what you're doing, and how you're doing it. It's how you choose to handle these remarks that will determine the aftermath of these encounters. It's always refreshing to know that every action does not deserve a reaction. Just because someone addresses you, does not mean that it's even worthy of a response. That's how you get into trouble, by entertaining chaos and conversations full of negativity and garbage. Those things cannot go with you on your journey. They will weigh you down, and it will end up being very costly. It's no different than hauling around a past that no longer applies to you.

Keep your thoughts clear, and refrain from entertaining anything doubtful. To pray and worry or to say that you have faith and also worry, would make you double minded, right? You can't do both. James 1: 5-8 Faith and fear cannot reside in the same house. Keep all the trash exactly where it belongs. In the trash can.

Step 2
Trust your process.

Set your mind at peace by focusing on the Lord, not others. No two people are alike in this world, and that's the beauty of the whole process. Grab a hold of all the gifts and talents that the Lord has given you and use them to your fullest capabilities. Your gifts will make room for you and take you before great men. However, it's your character that will keep you there. Don't let rough patches or trials alter your attitude or character. Don't allow disappointments to put you in such a deep place of overwhelm, that you stop *using* your gifts and talents, either. That only offers satisfaction to the enemy.

Having a bad day, week, or month, is not equivalent to having a bad life. Recognize that it's crucial for you to believe in yourself, and also to believe that you can use your gifts and talents to serve the Lord, as well as others. They might not look like the gifts of others, or even be received in the same manner as you see others being received, but don't be discouraged. Comparison is the thief of joy, and God does not want you to be concerned about measuring up to what anyone else is doing.

You are just as important as anyone else in this world, no matter who you are. It doesn't matter where you live, what color you are, or how highly educated you might be. You are important, and God does have a purpose for you. It could be raising your children, finding an organization, teaching, or even pastoring a church, but it does exist.

You will totally miss it, if you are concerned about what others are doing and whether or not you should be doing that very same thing. We've covered identifying purpose, as well as the downside of attempting to hi-jack someone else's purpose. So, at this point, you have to take ownership of what is for you. You must take full ownership of your process.

Everything that you face on your journey, is designed to make you stronger in order to be prepared for the situations you will face as an individual. Preparation is such a huge factor in order for you to stay in the places that God elevates you to. God does not just want you to obtain a thing. He wants you to sustain everything that He blesses you with for a lifetime. This is exactly why your individual process will be a very unique experience and unlike anyone else's. God already knows the plans that He has for you. He knows what you're going to face long before it's ever a thought in your imagination. He simply wants you to be ready. He wants to be sure that you don't get caught up in emotions, (which is easy to do), and that you stay focused on your vision.

Your job, is to trust that He has your back. On your worst day, you still have to believe that He will do exactly what He said. On your worst day, you still have to act like you have the faith that you claim to have. Don't be that person who only offers lip service, but can't follow through. You can't be all in when things are going good, and ready to throw in the towel when you feel a little turbulence.

The most rewarding thing about your process, is that

somebody who needs to be empowered, motivated, and blessed, is watching you. Someone is always watching you. Remember that. What's sad, is that so many people get caught up in focusing on who's "hating". Don't let this be you. Everyone is not hating on you. Some people are actually waiting to see you succeed. They not only want, but need you to win. Some people are just waiting to see a success story, period. Mainly, because their lives have been full of failure, and they need to latch on to a glimmer of hope somewhere. That glimmer of hope, could be you. Of course, you need to trust the process for yourself, but just keep in mind that it's not always all about you. Somebody is waiting to witness the success of your press.

Allow God to have His way in your life. Allow Him to show you the fullness of every blessing that has your name on it, by preparing you for your journey. Just drive. When you feel like things are getting a bit overwhelming, ask Him to take the wheel. He's got you covered. As long as you stay in His will… As long as you don't give up on the process prematurely… You will remain fully insured with paid premiums and no deductibles.

www.ingramcontent.com/pod-product-compliance
Lightning Source LLC
Chambersburg PA
CBHW070950180426
43194CB00041B/1998